Mom

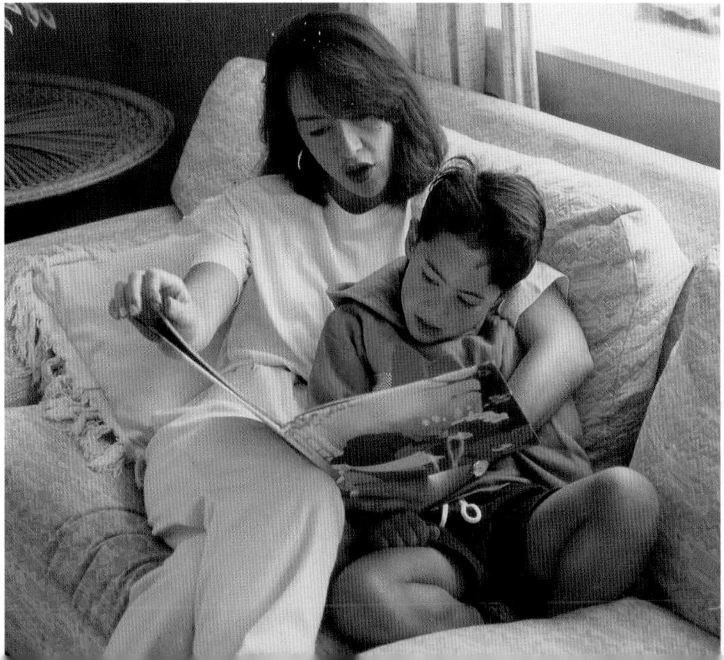

Mom is cooking.

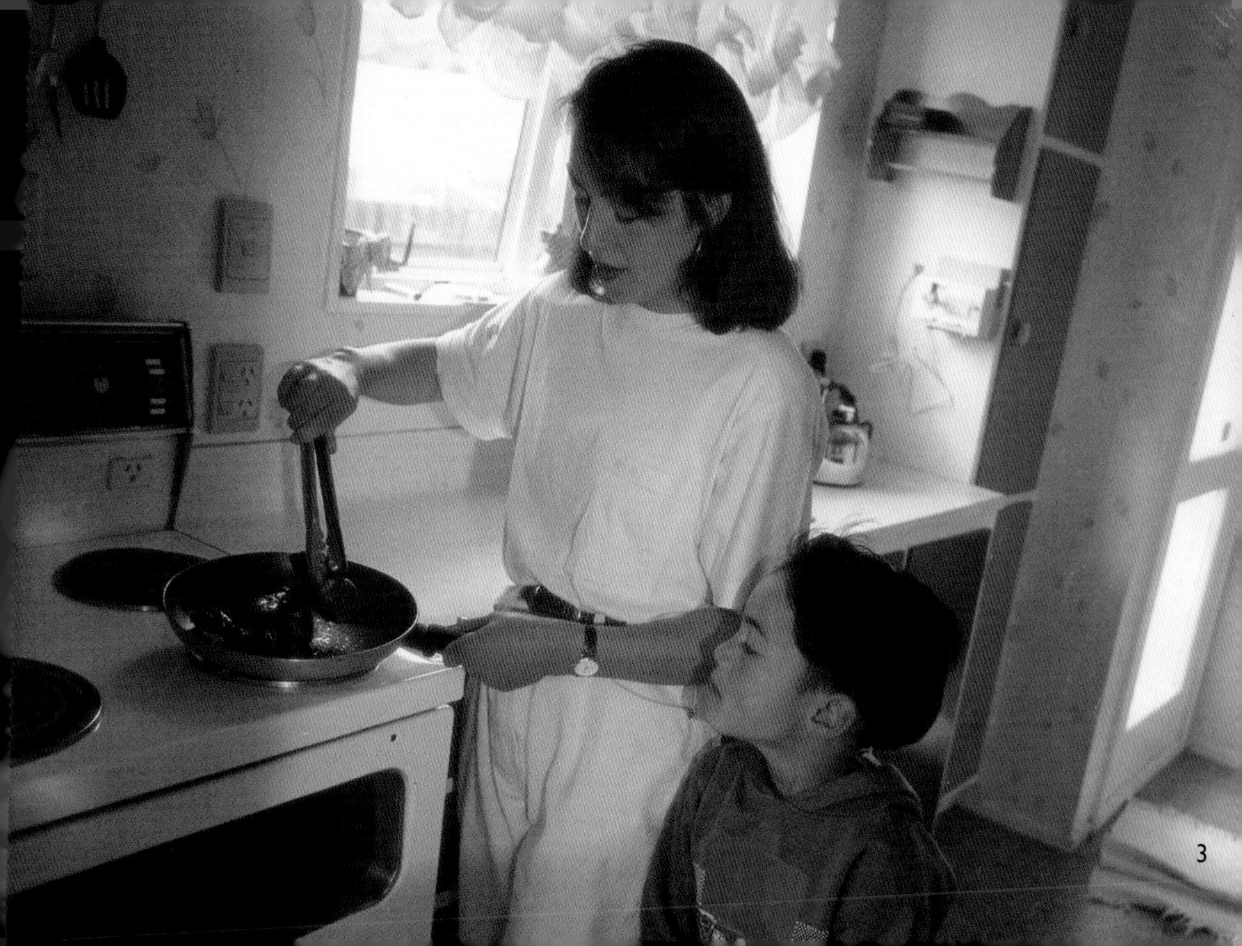

Mom is painting.

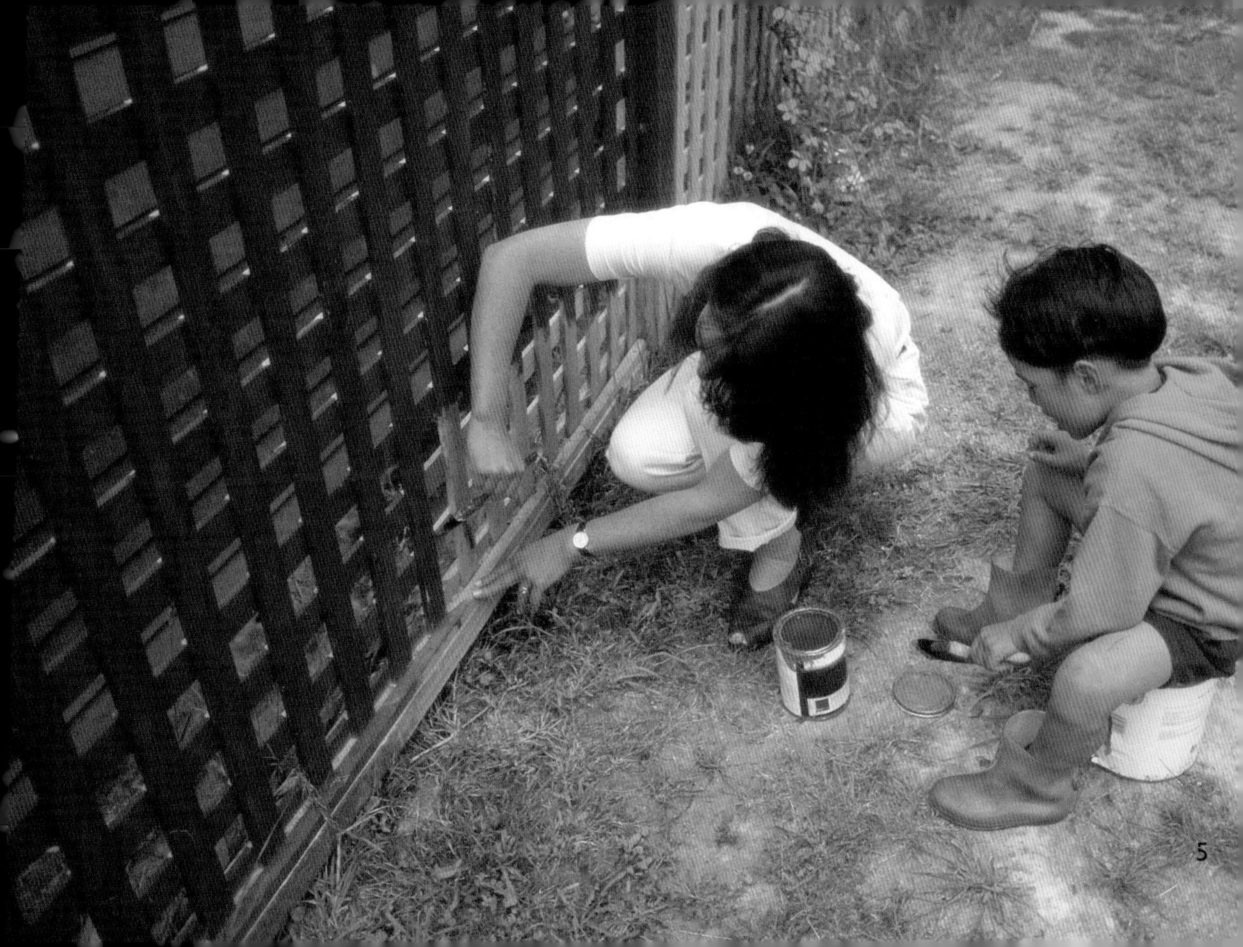

Mom is driving.

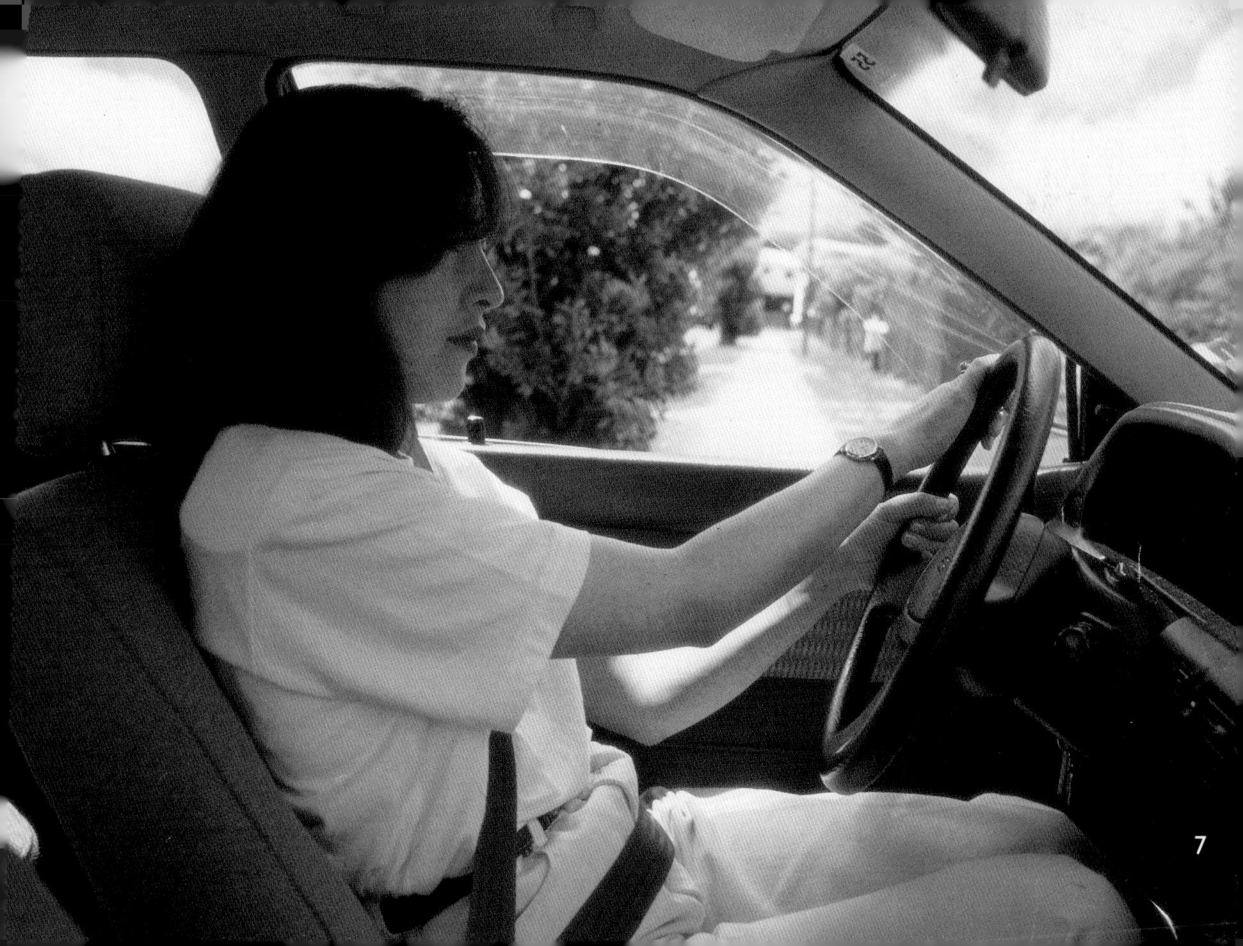

Mom is swimming.

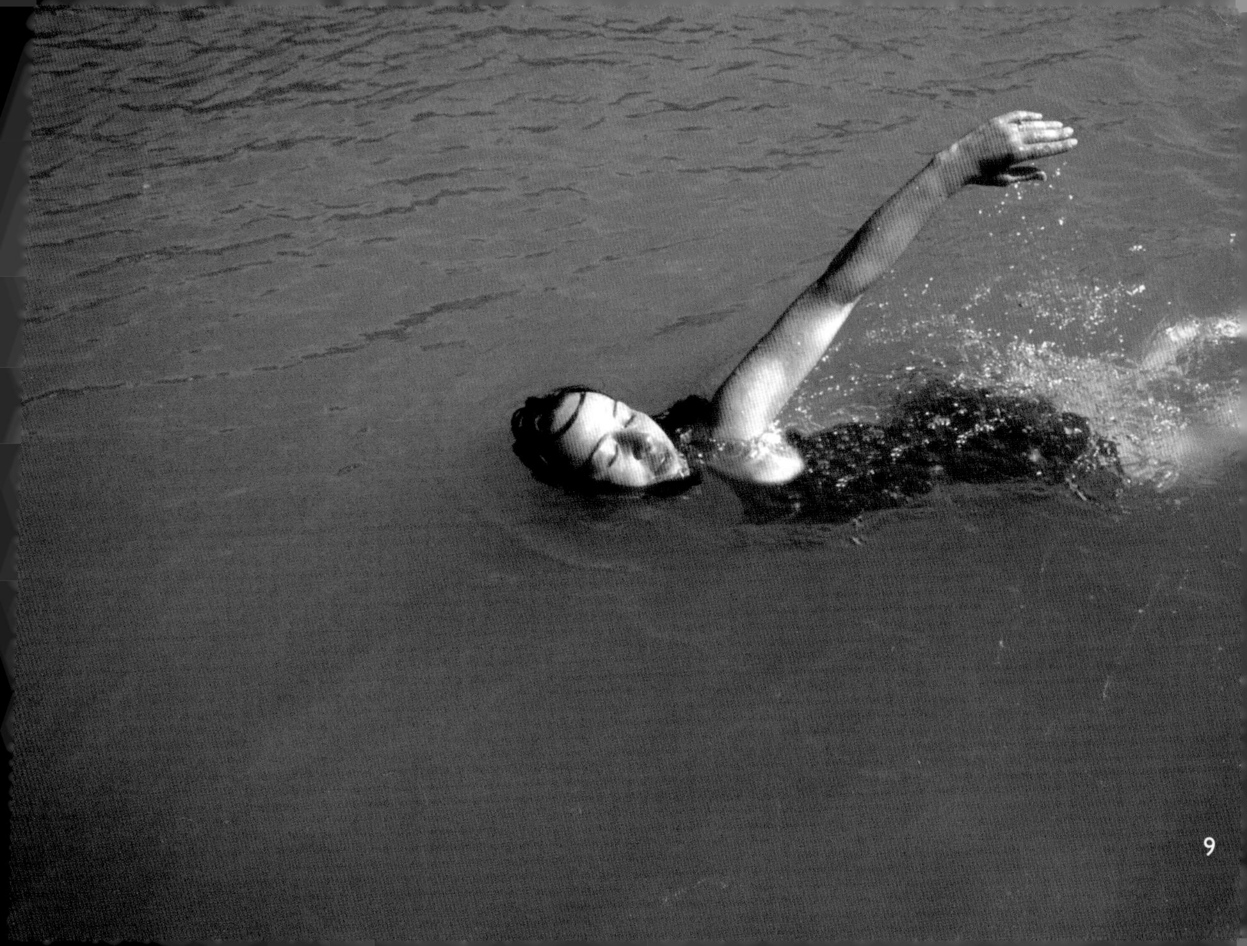

Mom is digging.

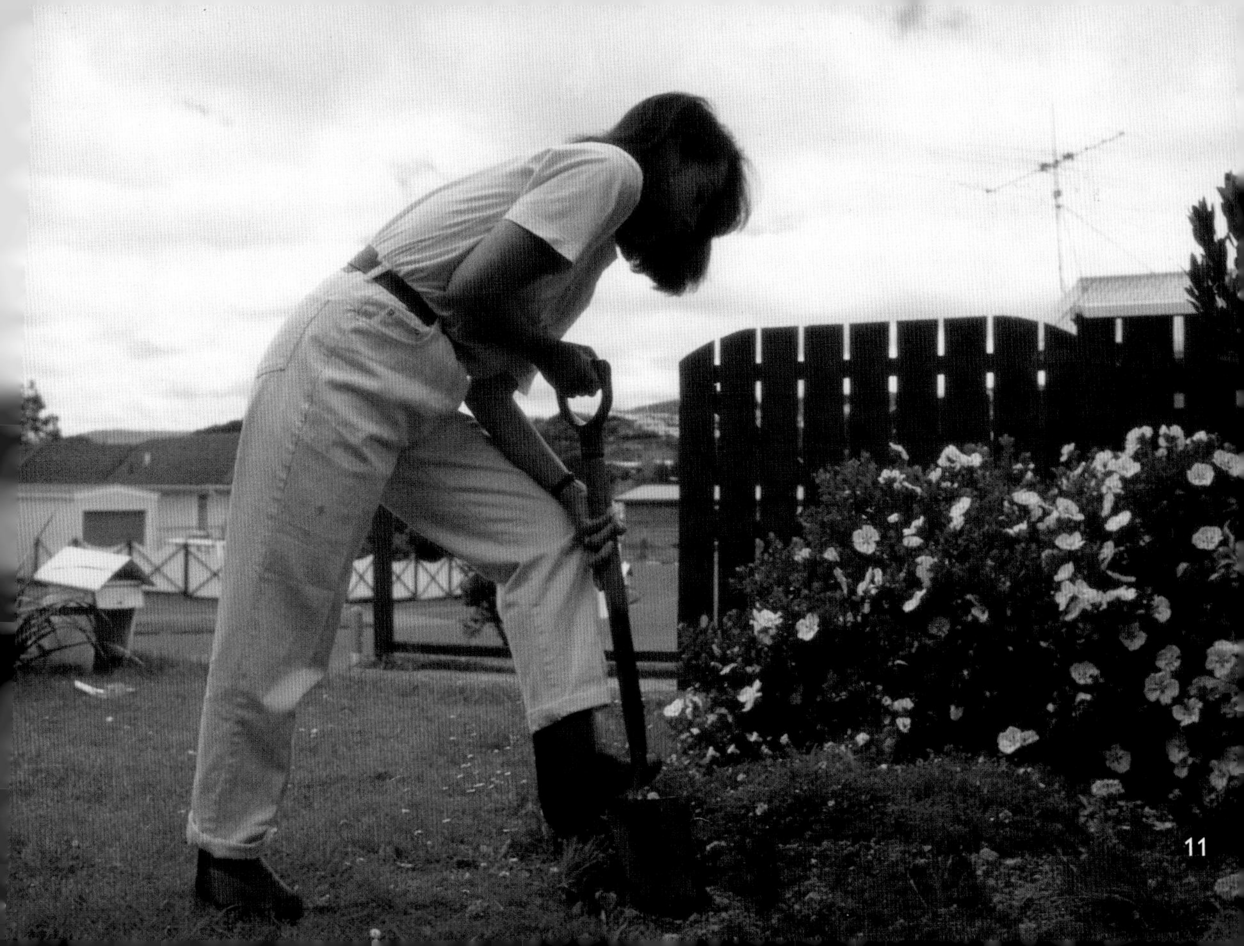

Mom is running.

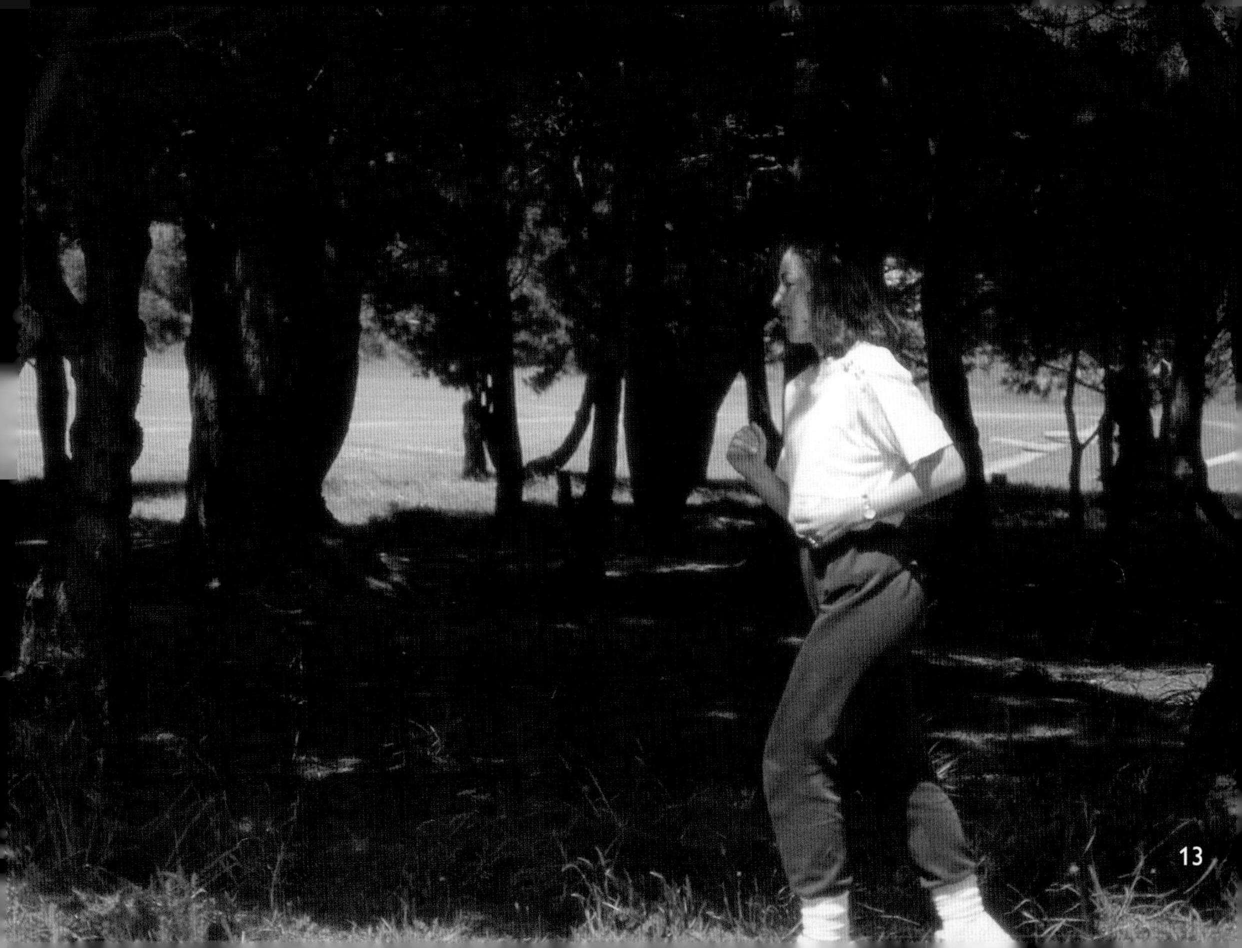

Mom is reading.

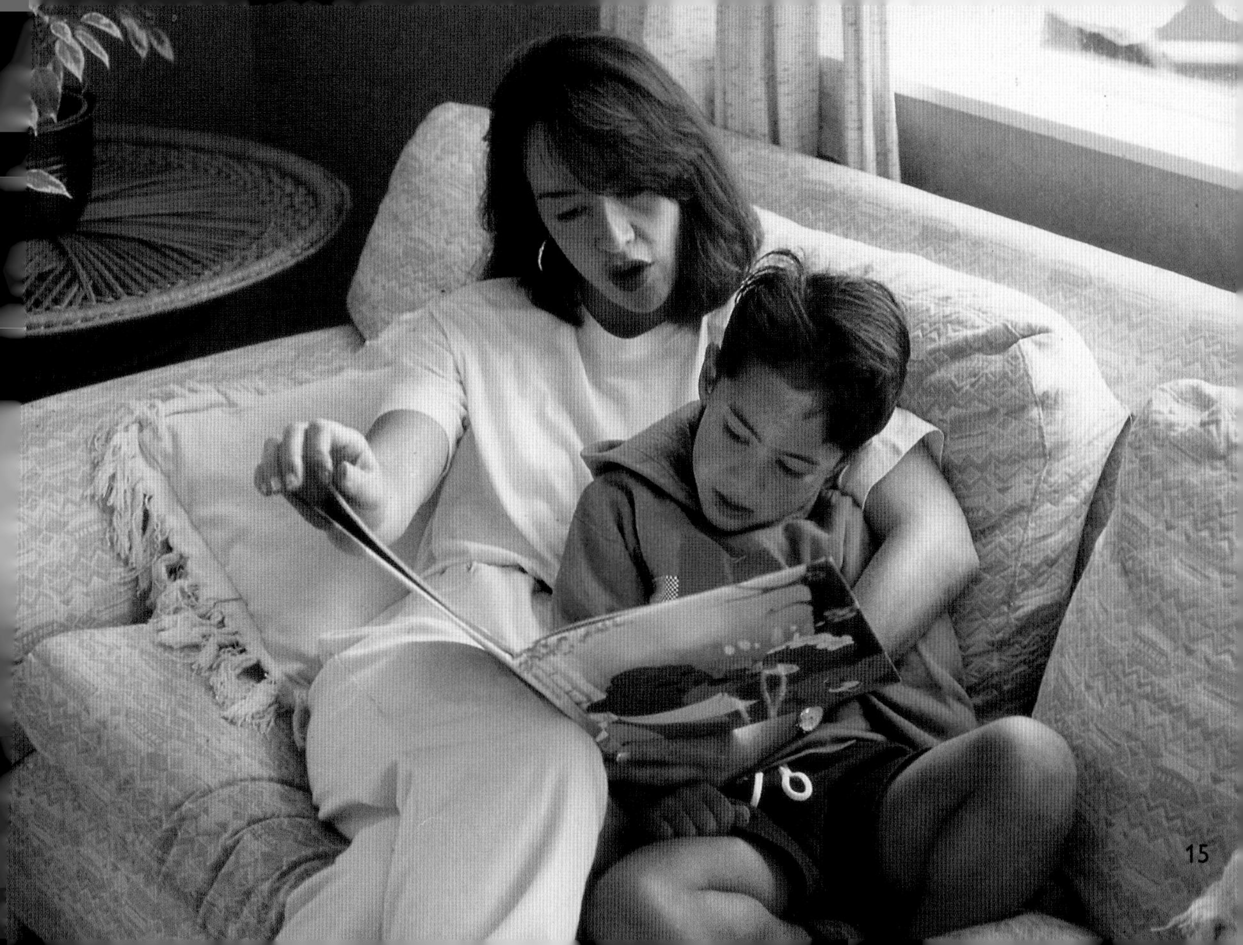

Mom is sleeping.

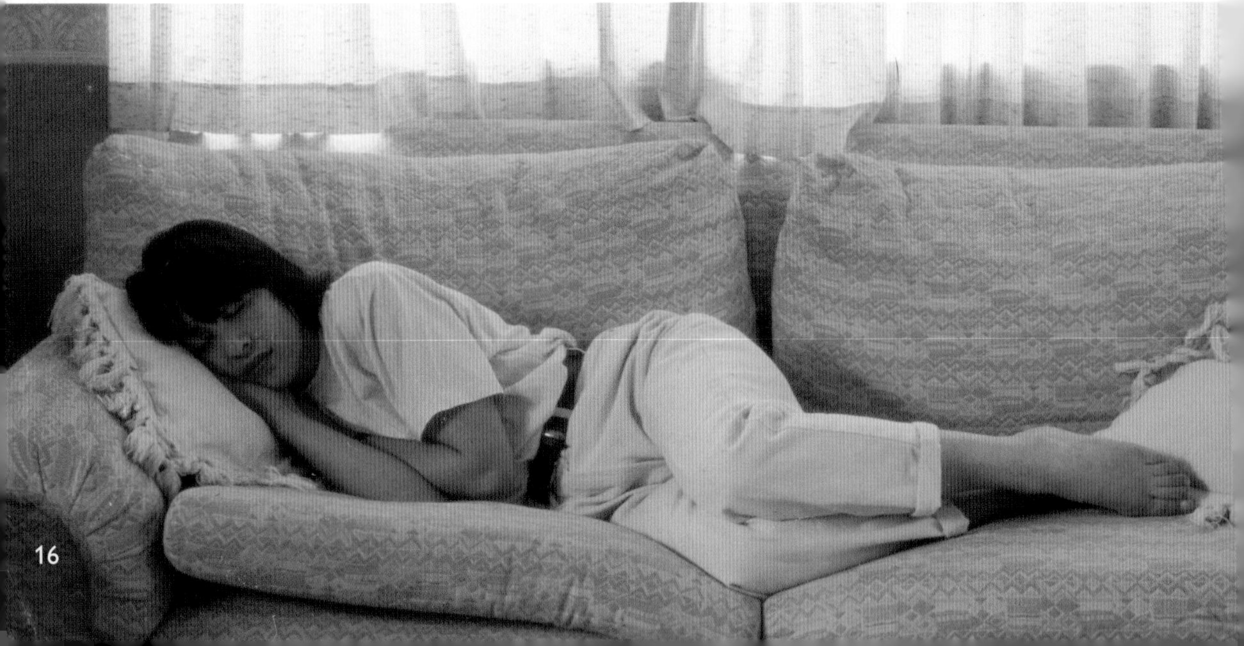